THE ABSOLUTELY ESSENTIAL
WRITING GUIDE
for *Kids*

A Reference Manual for:
- Writing Process
- Terminology
- Formatting
- Common Errors

Written by Nancy Atlee • Illustrated by Mary Lou Johnson

Routledge
Taylor & Francis Group

NEW YORK AND LONDON

First published 2005 by Prufrock Press Inc.

Published 2021 by Routledge
605 Third Avenue, New York, NY 10017
2 Park Square, Milton Park, Abingdon, Oxon OX14 4RN

Routledge is an imprint of the Taylor & Francis Group, an informa business

ISBN 13: 978-1-59363-040-9 (pbk)

Edited by Dianne Draze and Sonsie Conroy

Contents

Introduction

"Reading a full man ... writing an exact man."
Francis Bacon

People develop the ability to communicate through listening, speaking, reading, and finally writing. Their first experiences with speaking come through listening; their first experiences with writing come through reading. These interrelated communication skills form the foundation of the language arts curriculum. Writing is the means by which people express their thoughts, feelings, knowledge, and hopes.

The act of writing is a process that combines strategies and behaviors that can be learned. Like other curriculum areas, writing also has a specific vocabulary that defines its process. This vocabulary gives structure to the way authors think about what they write and how they write. As they develop the vocabulary of writing, students learn how to think and talk about writing in terms of its essential elements. They are empowered with a greater sense of strategy and control that helps them become better writers.

Teachers of writing acknowledge the strong connection between reading and writing. Reading determines how students see the world, while writing determines how the world sees them. Many of the best models of effective writing are the authors of the stories and books students read. Through the study of literature, students learn to recognize different techniques, literary devices, and writing terms they can apply to their own work.

The Absolutely Essential Writing Guide is based on language arts programs that develop writing strategies and skills in a curriculum that puts emphasis on both literature and writing. Information is presented for:
- writing strategies
- four genres of writing
- the building blocks of writing: sentences, paragraphs, and essays.
- common usage.

Many examples are given to illustrate how terms and language are used, making ideas easy to understand and apply.

This book is designed as a supplementary language arts text for students. In the classroom, it can be used by teachers and students as an instructional resource for teaching and reviewing literature and writing. It is also an excellent reference for individual students to reinforce ideas and terms as they work either at school or at home.

The compact dictionary format makes information easy to find. Reference pages provide quick access to commonly asked questions. Writing strategies, literary and composition terms – students will find what they need to support their writing in *The Absolutely Essential Writing Guide*.

1 Essentials of Writing

- Elements of Effective Writing
- Questions Successful Writers Ask
- Steps in the Writing Process
- Pre-writing Strategies
- Editing Your Writing

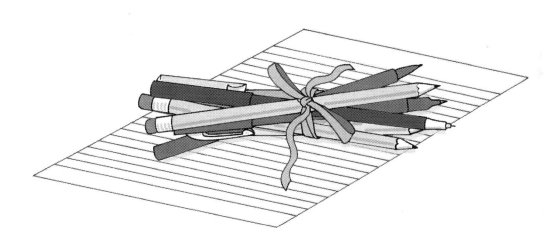

Elements of Effective Writing

The following elements provide a sound basis for evaluating the strengths and weaknesses of writing. When analyzing effective writing, note how the author's work reflects attention to each of these elements. When you are writing, check to make sure you have addressed each point. Most writing problems can be solved by revising in one or more of these areas.

Focus

Writing that has a tight focus is:

- clear
- concise
- purposeful
- understandable

Fluency

When writing is fluent:

- ideas are expressed easily
- transitions are smooth
- ideas flow

Elaboration

When writing has elaboration, it shows:

- development of ideas
- vivid impressions
- detailed descriptions and examples
- insightful thinking

Voice

When writing has voice, it is:

- personal
- reflective
- natural to the writer

Style

When writing has style, it uses:

- lively language
- strong action verbs and specific nouns
- varied sentence structure
- dialogue

Audience

The form of discourse, writing style, and use of language should be appropriate to the writer's purpose and the specific audience.

Questions Successful Writers Ask

Effective writers work with purpose and direct their ideas to a specific audience. This helps them make decisions about what they want to write and how they want to organize their ideas. The following are questions that successful writers ask themselves as they write.

Before I start writing

These questions help writers find a focus, narrow the topic, develop details, and organize ideas for writing.

- What is my purpose?
- Who is my audience?
- Do I care about my topic?
- What do I know or think or feel about my topic?
- What do I want my reader to know or think or feel about my topic?

When I revise my work

Writers improve a first draft by looking at their own writing objectively. These questions help writers make decisions about making the content of their writing better.

- Is my writing interesting? Will my reader want to turn the page?
- Have I said enough?
- Have I said too much?
- Have I moved too far off the topic?
- Are my ideas clear and flowing?
- Did I use strong action verbs and specific nouns?
- Does this writing sound like me?

When I edit my work

Once the content is set, after drafting and revising, effective writers edit for correctness. These questions help them edit their writing.

- Have I followed the rules for correct writing?
- Have I used consistent verb tense?
- Did I use noun/verb and noun/pronoun agreement?
- Are there any omissions or format errors?

Steps in the Writing Process

✏️ **Pre-write**

Get ready to write by (1) setting the purpose of your writing, (2) identifying your audience, (3) finding a topic, (4) narrowing the focus, and (5) organizing the sequence of supporting ideas.

✏️ **Draft**

Write ideas down in an early version called a *rough draft*. Work quickly to let ideas flow without pausing to consider spelling or punctuation.

✏️ **Revise**

Make changes to improve the focus, clarity, organization, and style of your writing. The ways to revise are:

▸ **Addition**
Add background, causes, comparisons, definitions, descriptions, details, dialogue, examples, explanations, illustrations, and information

▸ **Deletion**
Take out repetitive vocabulary, unimportant details, and awkward passages

▸ **Rearrangement**
Move words, phrases, sentences, or paragraphs to improve the sequence and flow of ideas
In dialogue, use a new paragraph to show when the speaker changes.

▸ **Substitution**
Change common words, phrases, and passages
Use active verbs, specific nouns, and varied sentence structure

✏️ **Edit**

Make corrections to improve accuracy. Proofread for errors in agreement, capitalization, expression, format, omissions, punctuation, spelling, and usage.

✏️ **Publish**

Share a final draft with others.

Pre-writing Strategies

What do you do when you need an idea for a writing assignment? Writers use certain techniques to help them generate ideas for their writing. When you are trying to think of something to write about, use one or more of these strategies.

✳ Brainstorm
List as many ideas as possible, working quickly without judging.

✳ Cluster
Map ideas around a central topic by connecting items to show relationships.

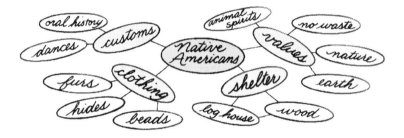

✳ Free write
Write for two or three minutes without stopping; let ideas flow freely.

✳ List, rank, write
- ▶ Brainstorm a list of ideas
- ▶ Rank them order of importance
- ▶ Choose two or three ideas from the ranking
- ▶ Decide on a sequence so the ideas flow smoothly
- ▶ Begin drafting

✳ Looping
- ▶ Free write about a topic for two minutes
- ▶ Stop and circle a word or phrase of interest
- ▶ Use this as a new writing topic and free write for another two minutes
- ▶ Repeat this process two more times

✳ Outline

Make a formal organization of ideas.

✳ Personal inventory

Make a list of favorite things that can be used as writing topics.

memories   thoughts   surprises   events
experiences   feelings   reflections

✳ Time line

Make a chronological list of events to help find a focus within a topic.

✳ Sketch and write

Draw a detailed picture, then turn it into a piece of writing.

✳ Writer's notebook

Make a place to record thoughts, reflections, experiences, bits of conversation, observations, and impressions for future use in writing.

Editing Your Writing

When you edit your writing, look for these common mistakes. By correcting these errors, your writing will become clear and easy-to-read.

 Agreement

▸ **Pronoun agreement** - A pronoun must agree with its antecedent in gender, number, and person.

Mrs. Sanchez sent her friends postcards from Hawaii.
(both third person, feminine, and singular)

The bears hibernated in their caves all winter.
(both third person and plural)

▸ **Verb agreement** - A verb must agree with other verbs in tense. A verb must also agree with the subject of the sentence in person and number.

The actors study their lines on the weekend and rehearse during the week. (both present tense)

After school they walked home, ate a snack, and finished their homework. (all past tense)

I talk on the phone to my grandmother every Saturday.
(first person, singular subject and verb)

Mary always wins the Monopoly games.
(third person, singular subject and verb)

The bike riders meet every Saturday at the park.
(third person, plural subject and verb)

 Wordiness

Omit words and phrases that restate what has already been said. Don't use many words to say what can be clearly said in a few words.

wordy	Have you completely done a thorough search for your missing keys?
correct	Have you thoroughly searched for your missing key?

Capitalization

Not capitalizing words that should be capitalized.

correct	Mr. and Mrs. Kim will visit the Louvre when they travel to France next summer.
incorrect	Mr. and mrs. kim will visit the louvre when they travel to france next summer.

Capitalizing words that don't need to be capitalized.

correct	Gina will be the next president of our garden club.
incorrect	Gina will be the next President of our Garden Club.

Misplaced modifier (also known as dangling participle)

A descriptive phrase placed too far from the word it modifies, causing confusion.

correct	I found my backpack lying under my bed. *(lying follows backpack, the word it modifies)*
incorrect	Lying under my bed, I found my backpack. (sounds as if the speaker lies under the bed))

Omission

Read carefully to make sure words have not been left out.

correct	The new twenty-dollar bill has many features that make it hard to counterfeit.
incorrect	The new twenty-dollar bill has many features make it hard to counterfeit.

Double negative

Do not use two negative words together in a sentence.

correct	I do not have any money left.
incorrect	I do not have no money left.

✏ Pronoun shift

The number or person of a pronoun should always agree with its antecedent.

▸ **Number of pronoun**

correct   Each girl in the ballet class needs to bring her own music tape to the audition.

incorrect   Each girl in the ballet class needs to bring their own music tape to the audition.

▸ **Person of pronoun**

correct   I wear a jacket when I walk to school because it keeps me warm.

incorrect   I wear a jacket when I walk to school because it keeps you warm.

correct   The children who are in band will be dismissed.

incorrect   The children that are in band will be dismissed.

✏ Punctuation error

Check all punctuation, making sure it is not misused or omitted.

✏ Spelling error

All words should be spelled correctly.

✏ Transposition

Read carefully to make sure words are not out of order.

correct   My friend and I are building a tree house.

incorrect   I and my friend are building a tree house.

correct   My mother moved the candy dish.

incorrect   My mother the moved candy dish.

✎ Using the wrong word

Use the correct word or form of a word.

▸ Form of the word error

drove - driven	froze - frozen	threw - thrown
went - gone	become - became	

correct   I have thrown out all my old toys.

incorrect   I have threw out all my old toys.

▸ Homophone error

brake - break   their - there   to - too - two

correct   The coach gave the players their uniforms.

incorrect   The coach gave the players there uniforms.

▸ Part of speech error

good - well   further - farther   envelop - envelope

correct   He can throw the ball farther than I can.

incorrect   He can throw the ball further than I can.

▸ Tense error

hike - hiked   run - ran   walk - walked

correct   Yesterday we ran around the track three times.

incorrect   Yesterday we run around the track three times.

▸ Wrong word used

it - it's	sit - set	teach - learn
than - then	lay - lie	later - latter

correct   Lay the money on the table.

incorrect   Lie the money on the table.

2 Prose Writing

- Strategies
- Devices
- Techniques
- Terms

When authors write, they make decisions about how they will present their ideas to the reader. They use many strategies and techniques to make their work interesting, to create a mood, and to hold the interest of the reader. By knowing these writing devices you have the same tools to create varied, stimulating writing. The following are definitions every good writer should understand.

Abstract word

An abstract word names an idea, category, or quality that cannot be touched.

courage   intelligence   love

Action

In literature, the action is the series of events that tells the plot of the story.

Allusion

Allusion is the hint of an idea; an indirect reference to an historical or literary character or event, a biblical passage, or a myth.

"The August sun rolled up, hung at mid-heaven for a blinding hour, and at last wheeled westward before the journey was done."

(sun ... wheeled westward is an allusion to Apollo, the Greek sun god — *Tuck Everlasting*, Natalie Babbitt)

Ambiguity

Ambiguity is a lack of clarity that creates doubt about the meaning or leads to possible misunderstanding. An ambiguous ending lacks a specific resolution.

Analogy

An analogy is a comparison that uses a similar relationship to link two items, two ideas, or pairs of words.

- ▶ Formal analogy

    sock : foot :: mitten : hand
    (a sock is worn on the foot; a mitten is worn on the hand)

- ▶ In literature, similes and metaphors make comparisons based on analogies.

    The sun was like an orange ball in the sky.
    (simile - *sun* and *ball* are both round)

    The book was a window to a world of make-believe.
    (metaphor - *book* and *window* both show a view)

Analysis (of literature)

Analysis is the examination of the elements of a story (character, plot, setting, theme) in order to understand how a writer used them separately or together.

Analytical writing

This type of composition examines how the elements of literature or poetry interact to create characterization, drama, mood, and theme.

Anecdote

An anecdote is a short, often amusing, story used to illustrate an idea. It is sometimes used to begin a speech or a personal memoir.

Annotation

Annotation is a comment or note of explanation about a literary work.

Antagonist

The antagonist in literature is the person or force that opposes the hero or leading character (protagonist) in a story.

Anthropomorphism (see Personification)

Anthropomorphism is the technique of giving human characteristics or abilities to animals and non-human objects; in literature, this is called *personification*.

Antithesis

Antithesis is using opposite ideas in the same sentence.

On my trip, I learned the highs and lows of traveling alone.

Argumentation

This writing technique involves using logical reasoning to develop a point in persuasive writing.

Authentic writing

Writing that is based on personal experience is authentic. The topic is chosen by the writer rather than assigned by someone else.

Beginning

The beginning of a written piece includes the first sentence, paragraph, or page of writing. It is designed to engage the reader and build interest. The beginning may include dialogue, description of setting or character, a dramatic scene, or a flashback.

Body

In an essay or letter, the body consists of the middle paragraphs where the central ideas are developed.

Caricature

A caricature is a character whose qualities have been exaggerated, sometimes as a form of criticism or ridicule; for example, an editorial cartoon.

Central idea

The central idea is the main idea of a poem, thesis of an essay, or theme of a novel.

- An example in poetry is the idea of grief expressed in "O Captain! My Captain!" by Walt Whitman.
- An example from a novel is the theme of coming of age in *Where the Red Fern Grows.*

Character

A character is a person or animal in a story. This is one of the main literary elements along with plot, setting, and theme.

Characterization

In literature, characterization is the development of a major character, showing changes in feelings and motives for his or her actions.

Choppy sentences

This is a series of short sentences lacking fluency and variety of style. These types of sentences can often be combined to make more fluent writing.

choppy	I went to the store. I didn't have enough money. I had to go home and get more money.
improved	Because I didn't have enough money on my first trip to the store, I had to go home and get more.

Clarity

Writing has clarity when the meaning is easily understood. Strong vocabulary, clear phrases, and a logical sequence of ideas contribute to clarity. It is an essential element of effective writing.

Cliché

A cliché is a common expression that is used so often it has little meaning or importance.

His disapproval came across loud and clear.

Jackson's luck went from bad to worse.

Climax

This is the point of highest tension, suspense, or drama in the plot of a story; a point at which the action of a story reaches its peak.

Coherence

Coherence means that ideas in a paragraph or essay have closely and consistently related ideas. Coherence provides logical organization of information. Ideas may be related by chronological time, order of importance, or parallelism.

Combining sentences

This writing technique blends two or more short sentences into one in order to avoid repetition and improve style.

original	Our school won the prize for the best marching band in the parade. It was the Rose Bowl parade.
revised	Our school won the prize for the best marching band in the Rose Bowl parade.

Composition

A piece of prose writing based on a central idea.

Concluding sentence

A concluding sentence is the last sentence in a paragraph that ties ideas together and shows their significance. In a persuasive paragraph, it may indicate action that the writer wants the reader to take.

Conclusion

The conclusion is the final sentence, paragraph, or page of an essay or speech; the resolution of a novel or short story.

Concrete word

A concrete word names a specific thing in a classification.

The word "chair" is a specific object; its general classification is *furniture*.

Conflict

In literature, conflict is the tension created by opposing emotions, personalities, or events that contributes to plot development.

- ▸ Internal conflict   person against self
- ▸ External conflict   person against person
  person against nature
  person against society

Connotation of a word

Connotation is an additional meaning beyond the literal definition of a word; often associated with an emotional response. For example, the word "contest" may create various levels of anxiety (challenge, excitement, or nervousness) for different people.

When Lawrence sat down, I could see that this chess game was more of a contest than a friendly game between classmates.

Definition

Definition is the meaning of a specific word or term; it may be used in writing as an appositive.

Hyperbole, or extreme exaggeration, is commonly used in tall tales.

Denotation of a word

Denotation is the literal definition of a word; it does not take on any additional meaning or connotation.

> The noun "contest" means a competition between individuals or teams.

Denouement (see Resolution)

Descriptive writing (see also Imagery, Sensory writing)

Descriptive writing uses vivid, visual language that appeals to the five senses: sight, smell, sound, taste, touch.

> When she lifted the lid of the bee hive, the sticky-sweet smell filled the air, and the deafening buzz muffled out all other sounds.

Detail

Detail is a sentence or paragraph that contains a specific definition, description, or example of supporting information that develops an idea.

Dialect (see also Slang)

Dialect is an expression of speech, use of grammar, or pronunciation that is specific to a particular region or country.

> Y'all come back and visit soon.

Dialogue

Dialogue is the written conversation between two or more characters.

> "You'll come too, won't you?" asked Ellie.
> "Well, I want to come," replied Tom, "but I'll have to see if I can get someone else to do my paper route."
> Gracie added, "Try to make it. It won't be any fun if you can't come."

Diction

Diction is the choice of words in writing and speech; for example, dialect, formal, or slang. An author will use a particular type of diction to make the characters seem more authentic to the time or setting of the story.

Dilemma

A dilemma is a position of having to choose between two difficult or undesirable actions. In literature this device is used to create suspense or tension.

Dynamic character

In literature, a dynamic character is one who faces challenges that result in a change of ideas, feelings, actions, relationships, or motives; often the protagonist.

Elaboration

Elaboration is the development of a central idea. In expository paragraph and essay writing, the central idea is supported with facts, related ideas, examples, quotations, and details. In poetry and expressive writing, description, imagery, and sensory details contribute to the elaboration of the central idea.

Emphasis

Emphasis is giving added stress to a specific word, phrase, or idea to increase its importance; often indicated by italics.

I *don't* know what to pack for the trip.

Exaggeration (see also Hyperbole)

Exaggeration is any enlargement or overstatement of the truth; overemphasis.

The baby cried his eyes out.

I was so embarrassed that I almost died.

Example

An example is a particular fact or event that illustrates an idea.

At the beach I love water sports like surfing.

You could begin with the easiest tasks; for example, putting your games back on the shelf.

Exposition

This form of writing informs or explains an idea, opinion, or analysis; often formal in tone.

Expressive writing

Expressive writing has vivid descriptions that convey personal feelings and sensory impressions.

> I knew I had won the race when saw my coach running toward me, wildly flinging her arms, her words lost in the cheers of the crowd. I tried to breathe, but each breath was choked with feelings of pride and relief.

Extended idea

An extended idea is a definition or description of an idea developed through extensive use of detail and example.

Falling action (see Resolution)

Figurative language

Figurative language is the general term given to the use of figures of speech that extend meaning and images beyond their literal definitions.

> The long white fingers of the moon drew arching lines across the shimmering surface of the lake.
>
> (personification helps create the image of moonbeams)

Figure of speech

A figure of speech is an expression that makes a comparison or suggests a meaning beyond a literal interpretation. Examples are idiom, metaphor, metonymy, personification, and simile.

First person (see also Point of view)

The person speaking or writing is the first person. In literature, a story written in the first person is a subjective point of view where the narrator tells the story giving a personal perspective using pronouns *I, we, us, our*.

Flashback

A flashback is a temporary interruption in the narrative of a story to show events that occurred at an earlier time.

> She finished setting the table. As she looked at her grandmother's china, she remembered events of the last two years - the fire, the long journey on the train to Prairie Grove, and the beginning of a new stage in her life.

Flow

Flow is the logical, cohesive transition between ideas; the way ideas in sentences and paragraphs connect and relate to each other.

Fluency

In fluent writing, ideas flow smoothly from one to another.

Focus

Focus is the clear, sharp central theme or main idea of an essay, narrative, or poem; a narrow topic.

One Afternoon in New York
(title shows a narrow topic with tight focus)

My Two-week Trip to New York
(title shows a broad topic that lacks focus)

Foreshadowing

Foreshadowing is a suggestion of changes in events and mood that will take place in the future. Authors use this technique to give readers a hint of what will happen in order to hold their interest in the story.

Form

Form is the organization of ideas and structure of literary elements in expository writing, narration, and poetry.

Gender

Gender is a distinction given to nouns and pronouns: **masculine** refers to males, **feminine** refers to females, and **neuter** refers to things and ideas.

- ▶ masculine   Mr. Thomas, Robert, he, him
- ▶ feminine   Mrs. Joseph, Sheila, she, her
- ▶ neuter   cat, desk, intelligence, hope, it

Generalization

Generalization is a broad statement or conclusion drawn from a given set of facts; lacking in detail.

I saw a lot of interesting places during my trip to Dallas, Texas.

Hyperbole

Hyperbole is the extreme use of exaggeration to create humor or emphasis.

> Baby Paul Bunyan's strangest feature was his big, black, curly beard. Every day, his mother combed it with a pine tree.

Idiom

An idiom is a figure of speech used to show a common idea; also dialect or an expression whose meaning relates to a specific group of people or area.

> I had butterflies in my stomach at my first recital.
> (means was *nervous*)

> Let's hit the road.
> (means *get going*)

Illustration

An illustration is an example or explanation that makes an idea clear.

> An extended simile is developed in a longer text such as a paragraph, stanza, or poem rather than in a few words. An illustration of this device is found in Homer's *Iliad*.
> "As ravening fire rips through big stands of timber high on a mountain ridge and the blaze flares miles away, so from the marching troops the blaze of bronze armor, splendid and superhuman, glared across the earth, flashing into the air to hit the skies."

Imagery

Imagery is the use of vivid, colorful language that appeals to the five senses: sight, sound, smell, taste, touch.

> When the flood hit, the pent-up force of the roaring water surged over the levee in a torrent that engulfed everything before it in a towering mountainous wave — trees, houses, and barns creaked as they were pulled from the ground and carried away, disappearing in the water's fury.

Inciting force

In literature, the inciting force is the turning point in the plot development that creates conflict or tension for the protagonist.

Indirect quotation

An indirect quotation summarizes words spoken in a conversation rather than the exact words; not enclosed by quotation marks.

> Justin said that he would meet us after the game.

Informative writing (see Exposition)

Interior monologue

Interior monologue shows the thoughts of a character by inserting them into the narrative; interior monologue is put in italics rather than quotation marks.

> As she walked closer to the door, one thought ran through her mind: *Who would knock on the door at such an early hour of the morning?*

Introduction

The introduction is the first sentence or paragraph of a composition; in formal essay writing the introduction includes the thesis.

> You may think, like many people, that flying is dangerous, but flying in an airplane is actually safer than driving in a car.

Irony

Irony is the expression of ideas in a way that means the opposite of what is stated, often to create humor or sarcasm. In literature, it is the unexpected result from a sequence of events that creates a twist in the plot or resolution of a story.

▸ Verbal irony   A contradiction exists between what is said and what is meant.

▸ Dramatic irony   The author wants the audience or reader to know more than the characters in the story.

▸ Situational irony   A situation or event is the opposite of what is seems to be.

Issue

An issue is a controversial topic having more than one point of view. It can be an unresolved difference of opinion or feeling and is often used to create conflict between characters.

Literary present

Literary present is the practice of summarizing the events of a story in the present tense.

> Anne Marie fools the guards who stop her by pretending to act like her younger sister.
> (About *Number the Stars* by Lois Lowry)

Metaphor

A metaphor is a figure of speech comparing two unlike things that share a particular quality.

> The stars were diamonds in the sky.
> (stars and diamonds both shine brightly)

> Her lips were cherries, red and glistening.

Metonymy

Metonymy is a figure of speech using a characteristic of something in place of the thing itself.

> "The pen is mightier than the sword." (Edward Bulwer-Lytton)

> He hoped to get a white-collar job after he graduated from college.

Minor character (see also Static character)

In literature, a minor character is a supporting character who contributes to the background of a story.

Mood

The mood is the atmosphere or feeling created by the setting or situation of a story or poem.

brightness	gloom	mystery
optimism	pessimism	despair

Moral

A moral is a practical lesson learned from a story.

> Look before you leap.

> Don't count your chickens before they hatch.

> Good things happen to good people.

Motif

A motif is a repeated image, idea, or symbol that runs through a story or poem to develop the theme; for example fate, love, isolation, sounds, weather.

> In the *Iliad*, Homer repeatedly makes reference to the armor of Achilles and Hector to show their strength and heroism as warriors.

Mystery

A mystery is a set of unusual circumstances that needs an explanation. In literature, this strategy is used to create suspense.

Narration

Narration is the act of telling a story.

Narrator

The narrator is the person who tells a story from a first-person or third-person point of view.

Objective viewpoint

Objective viewpoint is the factual telling or reporting of an event, information, or story without personal opinion or bias. This viewpoint can be found in an encyclopedia or newspaper article or in a textbook.

Organization

Organization is the way information, paragraphs, and sections are arranged in a piece of writing to create the flow of ideas.

Outline

An outline organizes ideas using alternating numbers and letters that indicate relative importance of ideas.

I. Reptiles
   A. Lizards
   B. Snakes
      1. Poisonous
      2. Non-poisonous
   C. Turtles
II. Amphibians
   A. Frogs
   B. Toads

Oxymoron

An oxymoron uses two words with opposite meanings together to create an effect.

larger half	clearly confused	friendly takeover
silent scream	old news	tragic comedy

Paradox

A paradox consists of ideas that seem to contradict each other, yet state a fact.

The longer I sleep, the more tired I get.

The harder I work, the more I get behind.

Parallelism

Parallelism is an expression of similar ideas (words, phrases, sentences, paragraphs) in similar form.

On our trip we camped, hiked, and fished in the lake.

Before you leave, please put the books away, make the bed, and turn off the light.

The dog has learned to fetch the newspaper and to sleep in his bed.

Paragraph

A paragraph is a group of related sentences that develop one topic. Paragraphs in factual writing have a thesis sentence that states the main idea of the paragraph and several supporting sentences. In dialogue, a paragraph is the words of one speaker.

Personification

Personification is a figure of speech that gives human qualities to non-human objects or animals.

The sun opened its eye upon the sleeping valley.

The harvest moon, dressed in its finest orange garment, peeked over the hill.

Perspective (see Point of view)

Persuasive writing

The purpose of persuasive writing is to influence the ideas of others through logical arguments and ideas.

Plagiarism

Plagiarism is passing off the writing of someone else as one's own without giving credit to the source.

Plot

Plot is the way an author arranges the series of events that make up a story. It is one of the main literary elements, with character, setting, and theme.

Plot development

Plot development is the way an author uses the structure of a plot – the inciting force, conflict, tension or suspense, climax, and resolution of the conflict – to develop the central idea and characterization.

Poetic justice

Poetic justice is plot resolution where good or evil are rewarded in an ironically appropriate manner.

Poetry

Poetry is a form of expressive writing rich in emotion, form, language, rhythm, and sound; organized in lines and stanzas.

Point of view (see also first person, third person)

Point of view is the perspective an author uses to tell a story.

- ▶ **First person** - A character in the story narrates to create a personal interpretation of events.
- ▶ **Third person limited** - An outside narrator's viewpoint and comments focus on one character.
- ▶ **Third person omniscient** - An outside narrator's viewpoint and comments have an unlimited focus that may go to any character or event.
- ▶ **Objective** - An external perspective shows what is done, said, and heard without narrator commentary or insight into characters.

Prose

Prose writing organizes sentences and paragraphs in a way that is like everyday speech. As opposed to poetry that organizes ideas in lines and stanzas, prose is written in sentences of varying lengths and rhythm.

Protagonist

In literature, the protagonist, is the central character or hero in the conflict of a story; opposed by an antagonist.

Purpose

The purpose of a written piece is the goal the writer hopes to achieve; for example, to entertain, to inform, or to persuade.

Quotation

A quotation is the exact words spoken in conversation or a passage taken from a written source such as a book, article, poem, or song. It is set off from the rest of a sentence by quotation marks.

"Don't be such a bully," she shouted, firmly placing her clenched fists on her hips and squaring her shoulders. "I won't let you push us around."

Redundancy

Redundancy is the needless repetition of an idea.

I want to go to the beach immediately as soon as possible.

He collected the money and the funds from the bake sale.

Reflection

Reflection is a personal opinion or feeling about an idea or event; the result of deliberate thought.

Resolution

In plot development, resolution is the final action of a story that takes place after the tension of the climax is over. It is sometimes referred to as *denouement* or *falling action*.

Rising action

In plot development, rising action is the conflict, suspense, or tension that leads to the climax of a story.

Sarcasm

Sarcasm is an ironic or satirical expression with a bitter or critical intent.

"You're so graceful," my sister laughed
as I fell off my skateboard.

Satire

In this literary form, customs, people, or ideas are criticized or ridiculed through the use of such elements as humor, hyperbole, irony, and sarcasm.

Animal Farm   *The Phantom Tollbooth*

Second person

Second person is the person to whom an expression is addressed, using pronouns *you, your, yours.*

Sensory writing

Sensory writing is descriptive language that appeals to the five senses: seeing, hearing, touching, smelling, tasting.

When she took a bite, the chocolate coated her
mouth, spreading its creamy, bitter-sweet taste.
Its smell, rich and earth-like, was almost as good
as its taste.

Sentence combining (see Combining sentences)

Sequence

The order of continuous or connected events in sentences, paragraphs, and stories forms the sequence.

Setting

The setting includes the time, place, and mood of a story. It is one of the main literary elements, with character, plot, and theme.

Simile

A simile is a figure of speech that compares two unlike things using *like* or *as*.

She can run as fast as the wind.

The moon was as faint as fairy wings.

Slang

Slang is informal, non-standard vocabulary and use of language. (see also Dialect)

Static character

A static character is a predictable character whose role in a story does not change; a supporting character.

Stereotype

Stereotype is the typical representation of a person or idea using uniform personality or characteristics; for example, the butler in a mystery or a nosy neighbor.

Structure

Structure is the way an author arranges the different parts of a sentence, paragraph, drama, or story to construct the whole.

Style

Style of writing is the type of expression and vocabulary a writer chooses to develop his or her ideas.

Subjective viewpoint

A subjective viewpoint is a personal point of view or interpretation that reflects the writer's feelings and opinions; for example, a letter to the editor, personal narrative, or a reflection.

Superfluous (see Redundancy)

Supporting sentence

A supporting sentence gives an important fact or idea about a topic.

Many types of spiders live in the desert of the Southwest.
(topic sentence)

One spider attacks its food by jumping long distances. Another spider is colorful enough to hide in flowers and catch butterflies.
(supporting sentences)

Suspense

In literature, suspense is used to hold a reader's interest in what, how, and why events will happen. This writing technique contributes to plot development.

Symbol

A symbol is someone or something that represents or suggests something else; a dove is a symbol of peace.

Tension

In literature, tension is the stress created by conflict between characters or events that contributes to plot development.

Theme

The theme is the intended message of a writer. In literature, it is the central idea of a story or poem and is one of the main literary elements along with character, plot, and setting.

Thesis

The main idea or point of view developed in writing is the thesis.

Thesis sentence

A thesis sentence is an introductory sentence that explains the purpose and main ideas of an essay.

Third person (see also Point of View)

The third person is the person or thing being spoken about. In literature written in the third person, the narrator is outside the action of the story giving an overall perspective, using the pronouns *he, she, it, they*.

Tightening

Tightening involves deleting text that is redundant, wordy, or off the topic in order to strengthen the focus.

Tone

Tone is the attitude of a writer toward a subject. For example, the tone could be critical, humorous, ironic, serious, or supportive.

Topic

The topic is the idea a person chooses to write about.

Topic sentence

A topic sentence states the main idea in a paragraph; it is often the first sentence.

Topic shift

A topic shift changes the topic and requires a new paragraph.

Transition (see also Reference, Transitions, page 74)

A transition is a word, phrase, or sentence used to smooth the connection between two ideas or show their relationship.

first of all	secondly	finally
as a result	however	therefore

Unity

Unity in writing means using supporting sentences and details that help develop a main idea and bring cohesion to writing by keeping ideas relevant to the focus of the writing.

Usage

Usage is the way a word or phrase is used in speaking or writing to show meaning, tense, voice, and tone.

Variety

Writing with variety means using different vocabulary and sentence structure to improve the writing style.

Voice

Voice is a reflection of the author's ideas, tone, and style.

Voice shift

This is a writing error that changes the person of the narrator; for example, from *I* to *you,* in the same sentence, paragraph, or story.

Wordiness

This writing error involves using unnecessary words, phrases, or details.

correct	Without a doubt, everyone thought his excuse was unacceptable.
incorrect	By the way, there is no doubt that everyone who was there thought the reason he gave was an unacceptable one.

3 Fiction

Fiction is an imaginative narrative, created by a storyteller, as opposed to the factual telling of events. The following terms describe different genres of fictional writing.

Allegory

A story illustrating ideas about human values, such as truth or goodness, told through symbolic characters, objects, and events; often used in early church drama.

Comedy

A story told in a light, humorous, or satiric tone or manner; for example, *Tales of a Fourth Grade Nothing*, *The Phantom Tollbooth* or *Much Ado About Nothing*.

Drama

A story written in prose or verse to be performed by actors before an audience; a play.

Epic poem

A long narrative poem that portrays the adventures of a legendary or heroic figure like *Beowulf*, *The Odyssey*, or *The Song of Hiawatha*.

Fable

A story that illustrates or reinforces a helpful lesson about life (a moral); for example, "The Lion and the Mouse" from Aesop's fables. Characters are often animals that speak and act like humans.

Fairy tale

A story of fantasy that uses characters such as princesses, fairies, wizards, and dragons like *Beauty and the Beast*, *Cinderella*, or *Snow White*. Fairy tales often include magic and happy endings.

Fantasy

An imaginative story that includes unreal settings, events, and characters; for example, *The Chronicles of Narnia, The 21 Balloons,* or *The Lord of the Rings* trilogy.

Folk tale

A story or legend passed down from one generation to the next; part of the oral tradition of a culture or nation.

Historical fiction

A work of literature set in the past that reflects an accurate portrayal of events, characters, and the way of life during that period like *Amos Fortune – Free Man* or *Johnny Tremain.*

Legend

A story from the past, loosely based on an historical truth or myth like the stories of King Arthur.

Modern realistic fiction

A story set in present time that represents life in a believable manner. Examples are *Dear Mr. Henshaw, Maniac Magee,* and *The Egypt Game.*

Myth

A story of unknown origin, often about gods or goddesses, that explains a belief or natural phenomenon.

Narrative

A form of writing that tells a story; it may be factual or fictional.

Novel

A lengthy work of fiction that contains complex plot development and characterization like *Bridge to Terabithia, The Call of the Wild,* or *To Kill a Mockingbird.*

Novella

A short novel.

Parody

A work of literature, often humorous and exaggerated, that imitates another work in order to ridicule it.

Realistic fiction

Literature that presents an accurate picture of real life.

Satire

A story written in an ironic tone in order to ridicule human behavior or attitudes like *Animal Farm* or *Gulliver's Travels.*

Science fiction

A story set in a future time with elements of advanced technology. Examples of this type of fiction are *Fahrenheit 451, The White Mountains* series, and *A Wrinkle in Time.*

Script

A form of literature showing the dialogue and stage directions of a drama; usually a play.

Short story

A brief narrative; limited plot and character development emphasize mood or irony. Examples are "All Summer in a Day," "The Necklace," and "Thank you, Ma'am."

Tall tale

A tale with exaggerated characters who reflect a way of life like the stories of Pecos Bill, Paul Bunyan, and John Henry.

4 Nonfiction

Types of Nonfiction

A nonfiction piece of writing is a work based on fact rather than an imaginative work. Nonfiction includes the following writing forms.

Advertisement
Written or spoken public announcement; a form of expository writing often used in a persuasive manner to promote an idea or product.

Analysis (see also Analysis of literature, page 16)
An expository form of writing that reflects logical thinking in explaining the various parts of a complex object or process.

Article
A separate section or a piece of writing on a specific topic such as those found in encyclopedias, magazines, and newspapers.

Autobiography
The story of a person's life written by the person himself or herself.

Biography
A written account of a person's life.

Diary
A record of events in a persons's life; written on a daily basis or at regular intervals.

Directions
A set of instructions or procedures to be followed in accomplishing a task.

38

Editorial

A newspaper or magazine article written to show the opinion of the editor or publisher.

Essay (see also Essay Formats, page 68)

A written composition that analyses or interprets an event or idea from a personal perspective. Essays can be analytical, comparative, narrative, persuasive, or problem-solving.

Journal

A record of events, experiences, and observations kept by a writer as a source of ideas for future story ideas.

Letter (see Letter Formats, page 42-43)

A written message sent from one person or organization to another. Letters are generally categorized into two groups: those written for business purposes and those written in a friendly manner.

Memo/memorandum

A short note written as a record of an event or a reminder like a telephone message or the notice of a meeting.

Memoir

A personal narrative of a specific experience or event in a person's life.

Narrative

A form of writing that tells a story; may be factual or fictional.

News story

A factual report of a current event, issue, or human interest story published in a newspaper or magazine.

Note

A short informal letter like a thank you note; an abbreviated explanation or idea like research notes.

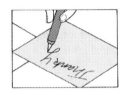

Report

An account of an event, experience, or study such as a book report, the report of a meeting, or a research report.

Review

A writer's evaluation of a book, play, or other form of entertainment.

Speech

A written copy or draft of a public address.

Summary

A concise overview of the important ideas in a longer piece of writing.

Correspondence

Terms and Examples

Closing

The closing is the sentiment expressed in a business or friendly letter before the signature.

Yours truly,   Sincerely,   Best regards,

Greeting (see Salutation)

Heading

The information given at the beginning of a business letter is the heading. It usually includes the writer's full address and the date of the letter.

Inside address

In a business letter, the inside address includes the full name and address of the company or person to whom the letter is sent; it is placed between the heading and salutation.

Salutation

The salutation is the opening of a business or friendly letter.

| business letter | Dear Sir: | To Whom It May Concern: |
| friendly letter | Dear Aunt Joanne, | Dearest Friend, |

Sample Business Letter

140 North Main Street
Dallas, Texas 75200
February 5, 2004

Customer Service Department
True Tread Shoe Company
411 South Main Street
Chicago, Illinois 60605

To Whom It May Concern:

    I am writing to complain about a pair of True Tread running shoes I bought last month. The soles started to separate after I wore the shoes just a few times. I tried to return them to the store where I bought them, but the manager told me to send them back to you.

    I am returning the shoes with a copy of my receipt. I do not want you to replace this pair of shoes. I want a full refund of my purchase price. Please send me a check for $59.95.

    Thank you for your prompt attention to this matter.

Yours truly,

James Smith
James Smith

Sample Friendly Letter

140 North Main Street
Dallas, Texas 75200
February 20, 2004

Dear Steve,

I have to tell you what happened to me recently. I bought a pair of True Tread shoes, and they started to fall apart as soon as I started wearing them. I had to send them back to the company.

Now I need a new pair of running shoes. What kind do you wear? Let me know as soon as possible.

Your friend,

James

5 Poetry

While prose is words in their best order, poetry consists of the best words in the best order.

Samuel T. Coleridge

Poetry is expressive writing that shows emotion, imagination, and reflection using verse form. Traditional forms of poetry follow specific patterns of rhyme, rhythm, and repetition.

■ Poetry Writing Terms

Alliteration
Alliteration is the use of repeated consonant sounds at the beginning of words to create a desired effect in poetry or prose.

slowly seeping   rough and ready   gentle giant

Anaphora
Anaphora is the repetition of words or phrases in lines of verse, usually to give unity to the structure of a poem.

So long as men can breathe or eyes can see,
So long lives this, and this gives life to thee.
(Sonnet 18, Shakespeare)

Assonance
Assonance is the use of repeated vowel sounds within words in poetry or prose.

breeze through the trees   time for a rhyme

Cinquain (see, page 49)
A five-line stanza.

Consonance

Consonance is like alliteration, but consonance is the use of consonant sounds anywhere within words to create a desired effect in poetry or prose.

sticky cookies   washed and brushed

Couplet

A two-line stanza. (see page 50).

The trouble with a kitten is THAT
Eventually it becomes a CAT.
("The Kitten," Ogden Nash)

Foot

A foot is the basic unit of poetry; different combinations of stressed and unstressed syllables in words and phrases.

- ▸ **anapestic**   ⌣ ⌣ / , as in the word *intersect*
- ▸ **dactylic foot**   / ⌣ ⌣ , as in the word *happiness*
- ▸ **iambic foot**   ⌣ / , as in the word *agree*
- ▸ **trochaic foot**   / ⌣ , as in the word *heavy*

Internal rhyme

Rhyming words that appear in the same line create internal rhyme.

Once upon a midnight dreary, while I pondered , weak and weary,
("The Raven," Edgar Allan Poe)

Line (see Verse)

Meter

Meter is the systematic rhythm in poetry, measured by the repetition of stressed and unstressed syllables in poetic feet. Meter is named by the number of poetic feet in a line.

one foot - **monometer**	five feet - **pentameter**
two feet - **dimeter**	six feet - **hexameter**
three feet - **trimeter**	seven feet - **heptameter**
four feet - **tetrameter**	eight feet - **octameter**

The meter of a line with five iambic feet is called *iambic pentameter*.

⌣ / ⌣ / ⌣ / ⌣ / ⌣ /
Shall I / compare / thee to / a sum / mer's day /
(Sonnet 18, William Shakespeare)

Octave

An eight-line stanza.

Onomatopoeia

Onomatopoeia is the use of words that sound like their meaning; for example, *pop*, *sizzle*, *whoosh*, *gurgle*, and *splash*.

> Isn't it funny
> How a bear likes honey?
> Buzz! Buzz! Buzz!
> I wonder why he does?
> (*Winnie-the-Pooh*, A. A. Milne)

Quatrain

A four-line stanza.

Refrain

A refrain is a line or stanza of verse that is repeated regularly throughout a poem, often at the end of a stanza.

> Cottleston, Cottleston, Cottleston Pie,
> A fly can't bird, but a bird can fly.
> Ask me a riddle and I reply:
> 'Cottleston, Cottleston, Cottleston Pie.'
> (*Winnie-the-Pooh*, A. A. Milne)

Repetition

Repetition is the use of a repeated word or phrase in lines of poetry, usually to create emphasis or mood.

> So that now, to still the beating of my heart, I stood repeating
> " 'Tis some visitor entreating entrance at my chamber door
> Some late visitor entreating entrance at my chamber door;
> That it is and nothing more."
> ("The Raven," Edgar Allan Poe)

Rhyme

Rhyme is the technique of using words or lines that end in the same sounds like *take/cake, maid/shade*, or *weave/deceive.*

Good people all, of every sort,
  Give ear unto my song;
And if you find it wondrous short -
  It cannot hold you long.
(from "Elegy on the Death of a Mad Dog," Oliver Goldsmith)

Rhythm

Rhythm is the use of a regular combination of strong and weak syllables to create a sound pattern or beat, like the rhythm of a limerick.

Scansion

Scansion is analyzing poetry to identify its meter.

Septet

A seven-line stanza.

Sestet

A six-line stanza.

Stanza

A stanza is the division of lines in a poem arranged by patterns of rhyme, rhythm, or idea; it is named by the number of lines it contains.

two lines - **couplet**
three lines - **triplet**
four lines - **quatrain**
five lines - **cinquain**
six lines - **sestet**
seven lines - **septet**
eight lines - **octave**

Triplet

A three-line stanza.

Verse

A line of poetry written in meter.

˘ ˘ / ˘ / ˘ ˘ / ˘ / ˘ /
If you wake / at mid/night and hear / a hor/se's feet,
(from "A Smuggler's Song," Rudyard Kipling)

Forms of Poetry

Acrostic

A form where the first letter of each line spells a word related to the central idea of the poem.

An army
Never stopping,
Taking bits of food.
Soldiers.

Ballad

A narrative poem that tells a story, often written in quatrains.

Priscilla on one summer's day
Dressed herself up in men's array;
With a brace of pistols by her side
All for to meet her true love she did ride.
(from "The Female Highwayman," anonymous)

Bio-poem

A poem about the life of a person; each line often starts with *I*.

I am Katherine Tyler.
I wonder how to fit into this Puritan world.
I hear the whispering sound of voices behind my back.
I feel alone, like Hannah's flower.
I cry for my lost home in Barbados.
I am the one left out.
(a reflection on Kit Tyler from *Witch of Blackbird Pond*, Elizabeth George Speare)

Sonnet

A poem of fourteen lines that expresses personal ideas and feelings. A question is often posed in the first part of the sonnet and resolved in the final lines.

- ▸ **English/Shakespearean** - three quatrains and a couplet in iambic pentameter with a rhyme pattern of *abab, / cdcd, / efef, / gg*.

- ▸ **Italian/Petrarchan** - an octave and a sestet with a rhyme pattern of *abbaabba / cdecde* or *cdcdcd*.

Tanka

A poem of five lines and thirty-one syllables, expressing pictures of nature and the seasons.

Silver drops of rain	(5 syllables)
hanging on winter branches,	(7 syllables)
turn to ice crystals	(5 syllables)
I wait; the warmth of the sun	(7 syllables)
turns them once more into tears.	(7 syllables)

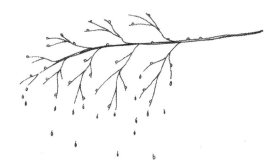

6 Sentences

■■■ Parts of Sentences

■■■ Types of Sentences

A sentence is a group of words that expresses a complete thought. All sentences have two main parts, a subject and a predicate.

■■■ Parts of Sentences

Clause

A clause is group of words that contains a subject and predicate. The two kinds of clauses are *dependent* (or *subordinate)* and *independent.*

▶ A **dependent clause** does not express a complete thought and cannot stand alone.

before our company arrived

because I like chocolate

▶ An **independent clause** expresses a complete thought. It may stand alone as a simple sentence or be used with other clauses in a compound or complex sentence.

The referee called the runner out.
(simple sentence)

I took my seat on the bus, and the driver pulled away from the curb.
(compound sentence)

After we roasted hot dogs, we shot off fireworks.
(complex sentence)

I like to do my homework after I practice my ballet.
(complex sentence)

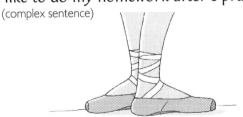

▶ A **non-restrictive clause** modifies a specific noun and is separated from the rest of the sentence by commas.

The chess master, who had not lost any games, felt confident he would win again.

▶ A **restrictive clause** identifies or defines a specific noun and is not separated from the rest of the sentence.

Lizards that are brown blend in with their surroundings.

Direct object

A direct object is a noun or pronoun that tells who or what receives the action of a transitive verb.

The dance teacher asked Ellie to demonstrate a turn.
(tells *who* is asked)

The frog caught the fly with its tongue.
(tells *what* the frog caught)

Fragment

A fragment is a writing error. It is a group of words that does not express a complete thought. It often lacks a subject or a predicate.

ran into the woods (no subject)

the girl with the red hair (no predicate)

while you were at the store
(dependent clause that does not express a complete thought)

Indirect object

An indirect noun or pronoun tells *to what, to whom, for what* or *for whom* an act is done; it usually comes before a direct object.

I sent Jamie a birthday card.
(noun - tells *to whom* the card was written; *card* is the direct object)

I also sent her a present.
(pronoun - tells *to whom* the present was sent; *present* is the direct object)

Phrase

A phrase is group of words that works as a unit; it lacks a subject and predicate. A phrase may be used as an adjective, adverb, noun, or verb.

Everyone on the bus got to school late.
(prepositional phrase used as an adjective to modify *everyone*)

We walked for a long time.
(prepositional phrase used as an adverb to modify *walked*)

The first person to score 100 points will be the winner.
(noun phrase used as a single subject)

Our team has been playing at the old soccer field.
(verb phrase used to show tense)

I like to visit my family in New York every summer.
(verb infinitive phrase used as a direct object)

Predicate

The predicate is the part of a sentence that tells what the subject does, is, or what happened to the subject.

Max plays saxophone in the band.

The puppies are outside with their mother.

The prize was divided among the five members of the team.

▶ **Complete predicate** - The main verb or verb phrase in a sentence and all its modifiers.

The fastest runners should run the last leg of the relay.

▶ **Simple predicate** - The main verb or verb phrase in a sentence.

The fastest runners should run the last leg of the relay.

▶ **Predicate adjective** - An adjective that follows a linking verb or verb phrase and modifies or describes the subject of the sentence.

His brother is smart.

▸ **Predicate noun/nominative** - A noun or pronoun that follows a linking verb or verb phrase and identifies or repeats the subject of the sentence.

The winner of the quilting contest was my grandmother.
(the noun *grandmother* follows the verb and means the same person as *winner*)

It was I who left the sweater on the playground.
(the pronoun *I* follows the verb and identifies *it*)

It was she who figured out how to solve the problem.
(the pronoun *she* follows the verb and identifies *it*)

Subject
The subject is the part of a sentence that tells who or what the sentence is about.

▸ **Complete subject** - The main noun or pronoun of a sentence and all its modifiers.

The winner of the diving contest collected her medals.

My friends and I like to play laser tag.

▸ **Simple subject** - The main noun or pronoun of a sentence.

The winner of the diving contest collected her medals.

My friends and I like to play laser tag.

▸ **Compound subject** - A compound subject has two separate but equal nouns or pronouns joined with either the word *and* or the word *or*. If the words are joined by *and*, the subject is plural. If the two words are joined by *or*, the subject can be singular or plural.

Hannah and Jake rode their bikes to the store.
(plural subject agrees with the plural verb *rode*)

Either Hannah or Jake has the treats for the meeting.
(only one person; thus a singular verb)

Types of Sentences

Compound sentence

A compound sentence consists of two or more independent clauses separated either by a comma and a conjunction or by a semicolon.

> I often bring my lunch, but my best friend buys lunch each day.

> The boys will line up next to the window; the girls will line up by the door.

Compound-complex sentence

A compound-complex sentence consists of two or more independent clauses and one or more dependent clauses.

> If we have a party, I will bring cupcakes, and Sarah will bring drinks.
> (dependent clause, two independent clauses joined by a conjunction)

> I can make the cupcakes, or we can buy some cookies if you think that would be easier.
> (two independent clauses joined by a conjunction, a dependent clause)

Complex sentence

A complex sentence consists of one independent clause and one or more dependent clauses.

> After we eat our snack, we have to clean up the mess.
> (dependent clause, independent clause)

> I would like to help you if I have time.
> (independent clause, dependent clause)

> While you were sleeping, James used your markers because he couldn't find his.
> (dependent clause, independent clause, dependent clause)

Declarative sentence

A declarative sentence makes a statement; it ends in a period.

> Lemons are sour.

> I like fruit salad.

Exclamatory sentence

An exclamatory sentence shows strong emotion; it ends in an exclamation point.

Oh! The present is absolutely perfect!

Imperative sentence

An imperative sentence states a command, invitation, or request; it ends in a period. The subject is usually not included in the sentence, but is understood to be *you*.

(you) Get busy on these dishes now.

Interrogative sentence

An interrogative sentence asks a question; it ends in a question mark.

Where are you going on your vacation?

Run-on sentence

A run-on sentence is a writing error. Two or more sentences joined with incorrect or no punctuation.

incorrect	I grew sunflowers Steve grew beans.
correct	I grew sunflowers, and Steve grew beans.
correct	I grew sunflowers; Steve grew beans.
correct	I grew sunflowers. Steve grew beans.

Simple sentence

A simple sentence is one independent clause, having one subject and one predicate.

Many bands played for the Fourth of July celebration.

Zach and Marcus are my best friends. (compound subject)

After the swim meet, the winners will be given prizes and photographed. (compound predicate)

Tommy and Gracie swam in the pool and played at the park.
(compound subject and a compound predicate)

7 Paragraphs

██ Sentences in Paragraph Writing

██ Sample Formats

A paragraph is a group of related sentences that focuses on one specific idea. Writing a good paragraph is the key to all types of writing: expressive, expository, narrative, and persuasive. Most paragraphs consist of a topic sentence, supporting idea sentences, detail sentences, and a concluding sentence. Transition sentences may be used to connect ideas within a paragraph or between paragraphs. These basic types of sentences (numbered below) can be used in a variety of combinations depending on the purpose, form of discourse, and audience.

██ Sentences in Paragraph Writing

There are five main types of sentences used in paragraphs. They are:

▸ topic sentence (1)
▸ thesis sentence (1)
▸ supporting sentence (2)
▸ detail sentence (3)
▸ transition (T) (may be a word, phrase, or sentence)
▸ concluding sentence (4)

Example:

(1) Today was my first day at my new school. (2) I wondered what my new school would be like as I got ready. (3) Even though my dad tried to warn me that moving to a new school could be hard, I didn't think so. (3) I'm a big kid, I thought with pride. (3) I would just march into my new classroom and enter third grade. (3) I dressed up in my best outfit, a red sweater and a blue skirt. (3) I stayed in my room for a while longer and thought about my new school. (4/T) Finally, I took a deep breath and ran downstairs to meet the school bus.

Sample Formats

If you can write a good paragraph, you can write a good essay. An essay is constructed from three types of paragraphs: introductory, body, and concluding.

Introductory paragraph

The purpose of the introductory paragraph is to capture the reader's attention and establish the focus of the writing. The introduction may open with an incident, an analytical commentary, a question, or a quotation. Ideas in the introduction should:

- engage reader interest
- establish the general topic and background information
- narrow the focus of the topic
- state the thesis of the essay.

The following three examples of introductory paragraphs are from *The Giver* by Lois Lowry. Each shows how a different format – incident, question, and quotation – can be used to introduce the same thesis ideas or central theme. Each of these paragraphs has three parts: (1) the opening, (2) narrowing the focus, and (3) the thesis statement.

▸ Incident format

(1) Jonas has successfully completed his training as the new Receiver of Memory. The community is depending on him to continue their tightly controlled system of government. Yet Jonas is on the verge of making a different decision that has lasting implications for himself, his family, and the entire social structure of the community. (2) In the novel *The Giver*, Lois Lowry explores the relationship between the individual and society through Jonas's character. (3) When Jonas becomes the new Receiver of Memory and begins to inherit memories of the past, he finds himself making a series of decisions that bring him into conflict with the values of the community.

▸ Question format

(1) How does a person face the challenge of a new and uncertain experience in his life? Does he hesitate and back away, retreating to a "safe" place where he is comfortable and in control? Or does he forge ahead into uncharted territory, taking risks even though they may result in lifelong changes in his relationships with family, friends, and society? (2) The direction one chooses can create a turning point from which life moves forward in a different direction, setting a new course for all future experience. In *The Giver*, Lois Lowry creates a tightly controlled world, where individuals face no challenges, have no choices. Society, or the community, decides all aspects of each citizen's life. Lowry explores the relationship between the individual and this society through Jonas's character. (3) When Jonas becomes the new Receiver of Memory and begins to inherit memories of the past, he finds himself making a series of decisions that bring him into conflict with the values of the community.

▸ Quotation format

(1) Jonas wrapped his arms around himself and rocked his own body back and forth.

"What should I do? I can't go back! I can't!"

The course of life is not a straight line. There are forks in the road, times in a person's life where he finds himself at a turning point, where he must choose a new direction. Once the choice is made, life moves forward in a different direction, setting a new course for all future experience. (2) However, in her award-winning novel, *The Giver*, Lois Lowry creates a tightly controlled social structure where individuals have no choices, face no challenges. Society, or the community, decides all aspects of each citizen's life. (3) When Jonas becomes the new Receiver of Memory and begins to inherit memories of the past, he finds himself facing a series of turning points that bring him into conflict with the values of the community.

62

Body paragraph

A body paragraph in an essay contains one of the major ideas of the central theme. It has a tight focus that is stated in a topic sentence. Supporting information and details develop the idea fully. In the following sample paragraphs (one-point, two-point and expanded paragraphs), sentences are numbered to show how supporting idea sentences (2) and detail sentences (3) work together to develop an idea presented in the topic sentence (1). The concluding sentence (4) summarizes and brings the paragraph to a close.

▸ **One-point paragraph** from the body of a narrative essay

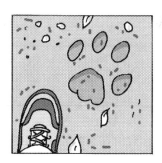

(1) My summer camp had a lot of new activities this year. (2) On the first day, we hiked through the hills and studied different kinds of plants. (2) An expert mountain guide showed us how to recognize tracks and signs of different animals. (2) We also learned how to pitch our own tents and build a safe campfire. (4) I knew I would have fun at camp, but I didn't expect to learn so much.

▸ **Two-point paragraph** from the body of a persuasive essay

(1) Our city should install a traffic light in front of the high school. (2) In the first place, a traffic light is needed for the safety of the students. (3) Several accidents have occurred each year, both before and after school when traffic is at its peak. (3) Even though a crossing guard controls pedestrians at the crosswalk, he cannot control traffic problem areas. (3) Students who are getting out of cars away from the crosswalk or riding bikes are often at risk. (2) Secondly (T), the traffic in front of the high school is causing a traffic tie-up for people on their way to work. (3) With a crossing guard, the flow of traffic is uneven. (3) Because there are so many pedestrians, he makes the cars wait too long, which causes a back-up around the corners. (3) Our school is located on a major street, one that does not have an acceptable alternate route. (4) We need a traffic light in front of the high school to control traffic in a safe, reasonable manner for both students and drivers.

▶ **Expanded paragraph** from the body of an analytical essay

(1) The irony in O'Henry's "Witches Loaves" rests in the character of Miss Martha. (1) Because she is both the protagonist and the antagonist in this brief sketch, the irony of the ending is inevitable. (2) As the protagonist, Miss Martha creates a fantasy personality for her customer; she sees him as an impoverished artist who lives "in a garret" and yearns for the delicacies Miss Martha sells in her bakery. (3) From her loneliness as a sympathetic spinster, come the ideas that she can offer him not only nourishment, but also encouragement and possibly even financial aid. (3) Her life takes on new interest; the blue silk apron and complexion cream symbolize her hopes for a potential relationship (perhaps her last chance) which she attempts to initiate. (2) At this point (T), Miss Martha becomes the antagonist in the story. (3) She convinces herself that her "suitor" is too proud to accept any direct offerings from her. (3) Even though she sees him get "thinner and discouraged," she resists giving an outright gift, not wanting to offend his pride. (3) Thus, "with a slight fluttering of the heart," she secretly puts butter in his loaves as a special treat to show her interest. (3) As she waits for his response, she contemplates his possible reactions to her overture. (3) The ironic reality of his reaction is sudden and swift. (3) "Ferociously" Blumberger attacks Miss Martha as a meddler who has ruined his project and his hopes. (3) Miss Martha realizes all further encounters with her "artist" are also ruined and resigns herself to the loss of her dream. (4) Her own gesture has dashed her hopes — she takes off her apron, throws away the cream, and resumes her drab existence.

Concluding paragraph

The concluding paragraph in a essay briefly summarizes, then comments on the significance and applications of the thesis ideas. The closing paragraph ties the important points of the work together and draws a conclusion for the reader. All questions should be resolved in the final paragraph and leave the reader with a clear understanding of the meaning and significance of the central idea.

The following describes two general types of essays and the techniques to finalize the central ideas.

▶ Analytical or informative essay

Explanatory, literature analysis, comparative, persuasive, and problem-solving essays are formal in tone and style. In writing a closing paragraph, writers choose from the following characteristics:

Transition

- introduces the conclusion
- brings the focus back to the thesis idea
- connects ideas from the body of the essay to the conclusion

Key ideas

- summarizes
- restates main points in a different, more powerful way
- reinforces the thesis idea using key words and synonyms

Application

- provides a sense of closure
- answers any lingering questions
- shows current or future implications the reader should consider
- reflects on the significance of the thesis

Opinion

- states the writer's opinion
- in a persuasive essay, encourages the reader to make a change or take action

▶ **Narrative essay**

The conclusion of expressive writing should be appropriate to the purpose and tone of the essay. A narrative essay may be less structured than an academic essay and may require several concluding paragraphs. In writing a closing paragraph or conclusion, writers choose from the following common techniques.

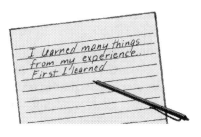

Circular conclusion

- narrative opens at a specific situation or place
- develops through a variety of encounters
- returns to the original place

Ambiguous conclusion

- withholds final resolution
- leaves unanswered questions
- challenges the reader to make more personal interpretations

Ironic conclusion

- events resolve in an unexpected manner, often with a twist
- uses understatement and restraint

Poignant conclusion

- creates an emotional response
- shows sadness or loss

8 Essays

■■ Essay Formats
■■ Types of Essays

An essay is an expanded piece of writing that uses multiple paragraphs to develop several ideas about a central topic. The purpose of an essay determines the specific format, style, and voice the writer uses. Essays can be used to analyze literature or poetry, to compare or contrast two or more different things, to offer a persuasive argument, to present a solution to a problem, or to introduce information.

Essay Formats

Though essay formats can vary, essays of all types have similar structural patterns:

- a thesis or central idea (stated in the introduction)
- a clear introduction
- several body paragraphs (often two to four)
- a meaningful conclusion

Essay formats also have similar writing requirements:

- clarity of expression
- cohesion of ideas
- logical organization of ideas
- detailed development of ideas
- variety in sentence structure and vocabulary
- correctness in usage, grammar, spelling, and punctuation

Types of Essays

 ## Comparative Essay

A comparison essay is used to compare and contrast ideas on two or three major points. A comparison essay may be organized into a four-paragraph or five-paragraph format.

Four-paragraph comparison essay

- Introductory paragraph that includes the thesis sentence
- A body paragraph that develops one idea in the comparison
- A body paragraph that develops a contrasting idea to make a comparison
- A concluding paragraph that evaluates the significance of the similarities and differences

Five-paragraph comparison essay

- Introductory paragraph that includes the thesis sentence
- A body paragraph that compares two ideas on one specific point
- A body paragraph that compares the two ideas on a second specific point
- A body paragraph that compares the two ideas on a third specific point
- A concluding paragraph that evaluates the significance of the similarities and differences

 ## Five-paragraph Essay

This format is used for analysis, persuasion, or comparison on three points.

- Introductory paragraph that includes the thesis sentence
- A body paragraph that develops one specific point (e.g. a point of analysis or persuasion)
- A body paragraph that develops a second point
- A body paragraph that develops a third point
- A concluding paragraph that summarizes the central idea and relates its significance in a broader generalization or to other applications

Narrative Essay

A narrative essay may be used to develop a wide variety of topics or autobiographical memoirs. The format of a narrative essay may be less structured than an academic essay: more ideas may be developed; the number of paragraphs may be greater. The narrative essay format still consists of an introduction, a number of body paragraphs, and a conclusion.

Persuasive Essay

This essay is used to influence thinking or persuade the reader to take action. The order of ideas in a persuasive essay may either build from weakest to strongest or start with the strongest, which is supported by the remaining ideas. The choice depends on such factors as the purpose of the writing, the strength of the arguments, and the amount of time the audience has to consider the ideas. A persuasive essay may be organized into a four-paragraph or five-paragraph format.

Four-paragraph persuasive essay

- An introductory paragraph that includes the thesis sentence stating the idea or action to be changed
- A body paragraph that states a reason for the change
- A body paragraph that states a second reason for the change
- A concluding paragraph that summarizes the issue and the need for change of thought or action

Five-paragraph persuasive essay

- An introductory paragraph that includes the thesis sentence stating the idea or action to be changed
- A body paragraph that states a reason for the change
- A body paragraph that states a second reason for the change
- A body paragraph that states a third reason for the change
- A concluding paragraph that summarizes the issue and the need for change of thought or action

 **Problem-solving Essay**

A problem solving essay is used to present a problem and its possible solutions. A problem-solving essay may be organized into a four-paragraph or five-paragraph format.

Four paragraph problem-solving essay

- ●◆ An introductory paragraph that includes the thesis sentence
- ●◆ A body paragraph that states the problem
- ●◆ A body paragraph that states possible solutions
- ●◆ A concluding paragraph that summarizes the problem and evaluates the options

Five paragraph problem-solving essay

- ●◆ An introductory paragraph that includes the thesis sentence
- ●◆ A body paragraph that states one aspect of a problem and its possible solution
- ●◆ A body paragraph that states a second aspect of the problem and its possible solution
- ●◆ A body paragraph that states a third aspect of the problem and its possible solution
- ●◆ A concluding paragraph that summarizes the problem and evaluates the options

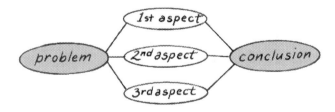

9 Reference

- Commonly Used Prepositions
- Special Uses of Prepositions
- Common Usage Errors

Commonly Used Prepositions

A preposition always relates to its noun or pronoun object. The following are the most common prepositions.

We parked the car across the street.
The broom was leaning against the wall.
They were warned to stay away from the construction site.

aboard	beside	into	throughout
about	between	like	till
above	beyond	near	to
across	by	of	toward
after	concerning	off	under
against	down	on	underneath
along	down from	on top of	until
among	during	onto	up
around	except	out	upon
at	for	out of	with
away from	from	outside	within
before	in	over	without
behind	in front of	past	
below	inside	since	
beneath	instead of	through	

Special Uses of Prepositions

Some verbs are followed by specific prepositions that establish a special relationship to the context of the sentence.

abide *by* (to obey a decision)

abide *in* (a place)

according *to*

account *for* (be responsible for actions)

account *to* (a person)

accused *of* (a crime or misdeed)

acquainted *with*

adapt *for* (a purpose)

adapt *from* (another source)

adapt *to* (a situation)

agree *on* (issues)

agree *to* (a plan)

agree *with* (a person)

alongside (no preposition)

analogous *to*

angry *about* (something)

angry *at* (a person or action)

angry *with* (a person)

apply *for* (a job)

apply *to* (a situation)

argue *for/against* (an idea)

argue *with* (a person)

arrive *at* (a decision or location)

arrive *in* (a car)

arrive *on* (a plane or train)

attempt *to* (do something)

based *on*

blame *for* (an action)

blame *on* (a person)

capable *of*

careless *about*

charge *for* (a purchase or service)

charge *with* (a crime)

choose *among or between*

come *to* (a conclusion)

compare *to* (something different)

compare *with* (a like person or object)

comply *with*

consist *of*

contrast *with*

convenient *for* (a purpose)

convenient *to* (a place)

correspond *to* (something being compared)

correspond *with* (through a letter)

deal *in* (a product)

deal *with* (people or things)

depend *on*

deprive *of*

differ *on/over* (an issue)

differ *from* (something being compared)

differ *with* (a person)

different *from* (not different than)

effect *of*

emigrate *from*

equal/unequal *in* (quantities or qualities)

equal/unequal *to* (a challenge)

excerpt *from* (a source)

forbid/forbidden *to*

identical *to, with*

immigrate *to*

in accordance *with*

infer *from*

inferior *to*

inseparable *from*

liable *for* (an action)

liable *to* (a person or authority)

opposed/opposition *to*

possibility *of*

prefer (one thing) *to* (another)

prevent *from*

prior *to*

protest *against*

rely *on*

reward *for* (an accomplishment)

reward *with* (a gift)

sensitive *about* (an insult or offense)

sensitive *to* (a situation)

similar *to*

substitute *for*

superior *to*

thoughtful *of*

unpopular *with*

wait *at* (a place)

wait *for* (a person or event)

wait *in* (room, car...)

wait *on* (serve a person or customer)

Transitions

Transitions are words and phrases that improve the flow of writing. By showing relationships that exist among ideas, transitions give coherence and unity to writing.

Chronology

at that time/same time
before
during
eventually
following
in the first place
in the meantime
later
meanwhile
now
sometimes
soon after
subsequently
thereafter
to begin with
until
while

Cause and effect

accordingly
as a result
as long as
because
consequently
for that reason
if
in order to/that
since
so that
therefore
thus

Conclusions

consequently
in other words
on the whole
therefore
to conclude/summarize

Conditional connections

although
even though
unless

Connections

again
also
for example/instance
furthermore
in addition
specifically
that is
the following
to illustrate

Contrast

although
but
compared to
conversely
despite the fact that
even though
however
in comparison to
in contrast
nevertheless
on the contrary/other hand
otherwise
rather than
unlike
yet

Degree of certainty

certainly
indeed
obviously
despite the fact that
even though
however
in comparison to
in contrast
nevertheless
on the contrary/other hand
otherwise
rather then
unlike
yet

Equal ideas

additionally
also
as well as
besides
in addition to
in like manner
likewise
moreover
similarly

Series

first
first of all
in the first place
to begin with
second/secondly
next
then
the next step
finally
lastly

Common Usage Errors

Usage errors occur when a writer is confused by words that sound alike, by different forms of a word, or by words that are simply incorrect in a given context. The following definitions distinguish between meanings and connotations of words that are often misused.

a - use before words that begin with a consonant
an - use before words that begin with a vowel

        I got a model train for my birthday.
        I ate an apple for lunch.

accept (v) - to receive, take, or hold something offered as a gift; to agree with
except (prep) - excluding
        I accept the terms of the contract.
        All the seats were taken except those in the last row.

adapt (v) - to change in order to fit
adept (adj) - skilled
adopt (v) - to select; to accept and put into use
        He learned to adapt to life in the wilderness.
        He is adept at playing chess.
        The couple decided to adopt a child.
        This is the schedule we will adopt for this year.

advice (n) - helpful information; recommendation
advise (v) - to give advice
        I asked my teacher for advice about my schedule.
        The principal advised us to take notes at the meeting.

affect (v) - to influence
effect (n) - the result of an action
effect (v) - to cause an action; accomplish
        Reading this article affected my thinking about global warming.
        The scientists studied the effects of the earthquake.
        In order to effect change, we must often take a risk.

aggravate - to make a problem or situation worse
irritate - to annoy or anger
        His absence from the meeting could aggravate the tension between them.
        The cat's howling irritates me when I am trying to sleep.

allusion - a reference, hint, or implication
illusion - a false impression of something that seems to be what it is not
> This poem contains an allusion to Apollo, the Greek sun god.
> A mirage is an optical illusion.
> The magician created the illusion of floating.

all ready - everyone or everything is prepared
already - before this time, previously
> The luggage is all ready to load in the car.
> I had already finished the shopping when you gave me the list.

all right - correct, good enough, acceptable; yes, O.K.
alright - incorrect
> I rechecked my homework and think my math problems are all right.
> All right, I'll go with you.

altogether - in all; thoroughly
all together - everyone or everything in one place
> There are altogether too many people in the elevator.
> The family sat all together around the dinner table.

a lot - many, very much
a lot - incorrect
> It will take a lot of paper to wrap this present.
> We liked that movie a lot.

among - use with more than two people or things
between - use with two people or things
> We strolled among the flowers in the garden.
> In math class, I sit between Julia and Jacob.

amount - a quantity that can be measured (e.g. in length, weight, time); the total
number - a quantity that can be counted
> A large party like this will require a large amount of food.
> The number of people in the audience was greater than expected.

ant - an insect
aunt - a female relative
> We watched the ant carry the crumb across the sidewalk.
> My mother's sister is my aunt.

any body - incorrect; not a synonym for *anyone*

anybody, anyone - any person (written as one word).
>   This applies also to *everybody, nobody,* and *somebody.*
>   Has anybody seen what happened to the garden?

anywhere, everywhere, nowhere, somewhere - do **not** put a final *s* on these words
>   incorrect - anywheres, everywheres, nowheres, somewheres

as - (see *like*)

ascent (n) - the act of climbing upward; a rise or advance
assent (v) - to agree to
assent (n) - an act of agreement
>   The ascent of Mount Everest was slow and dangerous.
>   The lawyer assented to the terms of the contract.
>   Do I have your assent on the plan?

at (prep) - indicates where something is or something happened; do not use after
>   *where*
>   correct - My sister is at the movies.
>   incorrect - Where is your sister at?

bad (adj) - not good
badly (adv) - not well done; poorly
>   I felt bad that I had to miss your graduation.
>   Because we hadn't practiced, our soccer team played badly.

bare (adj) - without a covering or clothing; unfurnished
bear (n) - a large animal
bear (v) - to carry or support; to produce
>   After we moved the furniture, our old house looked bare.
>   Put the food away so it won't attract a bear to the camp.
>   How much weight will the new bridge bear?
>   This tree will not bear fruit until next year.

berth - bed on a ship or train; a place for a ship to dock
birth - the beginning of life
>   The sailor stored his belongings under his berth.
>   The vet let me watch the birth of my dog's puppies.
>   On the Fourth of July, we celebrate the birth of our nation.

beside - next to
besides - in addition to
>The baby liked to sleep with her favorite stuffed animal beside her.
>What else should I pack besides the beach towels?

between - (see *among, between*)

blew (v) - past tense of *blow*
blue (adj) - a color
>The cold wind blew in from the Arctic.
>The blue of the ocean matches the sky today.

board (n) - a piece of lumber; a place to display information; a group that supervises or manages
board (v) - to get on a ship, plane, train, or bus; to cover with boards
bored (v) - past tense of *bore*
bored (adj) - weary of something after losing interest
>I made a bookshelf from this board.
>Put the message on the bulletin board above the phone.
>My mother serves on the board of education.
>We board the ship at 3:00 this afternoon.
>Before the hurricane, we were advised to board up our windows.
>The carpenter bored a hole into the cabinet.
>My little brother gets bored playing with his trains now.

borrow - take for temporary use
lend - give to someone for temporary use
>May I borrow your history notes so I can copy them?
>The library will lend reference books overnight.

brake (n) - a device used to stop a moving object or vehicle
brake (v) - to stop by using a brake
break (n) - a gap or opening of space or time; an interruption
break (v) - to shatter into pieces; make a gap or path
>Dad took the car in to get a new parking brake.
>The car braked to a sudden stop.
>We took a break after one hour of soccer practice.
>Our homes were saved by the fire break.
>Be careful; this fragile vase will break easily.
>The pioneers worked hard to break trails through the wilderness.

breath (n) - the air inhaled and exhaled
breathe (v) - to inhale and exhale
        My breath smelled like garlic after eating the pizza.
        When the air is polluted, it can be hard to breathe.

bring - move or carry to a person or place
take - move or carry from a person or place
        Bring your most recent painting to the exhibit.
        Remember to take your raincoat when you go to New York.

buy (v) - to purchase
by (prep) - near
        This year we will buy a new car.
        The keys are on the table by the door.

can (v) - know how or be able to do something
may (v) - have permission or the right to do something
        I can finish the report by 4:00 today.
        Mom says I may go to the movie with you.

capital - a city that is the center of government; an uppercase letter; money or wealth
        that is used in business or trade
capitol - buildings used by a legislature
Capitol - specific building where the U.S. Congress meets
        The capital of California is Sacramento.
        He invested most of his capital in the stock market.
        The tour of the state capitol will start at 10:00 tomorrow morning.
        This flag was flown above the Capitol in Washington D.C.

cent (n) - a penny
sent (v) - past tense of *send*
scent (n) - a fragrance or aroma
        I spent my last cent at the mall.
        He sent the package out yesterday.
        The police dog was trained to follow the scent of missing persons.

choose - make a selection (present tense)
chose - past tense of *choose*
        Choose a souvenir, and I will buy it for you.
        Max chose to stay at the hotel because it was raining.

chord (n) - a group of musical notes; a line connecting two points on a circle
cord (n) - a rope or cable; a unit of cut wood used for fuel (128 ft^3)
>Please play the C chord.
>He tied a strong cord around the package.
>We ordered a cord of wood for our fireplace.

cite - (see *sight, site*)

close (v) - to shut or bring to an end
clothes (n) - wearing apparel
>When you go out, please close the door.
>My mother always tells me to hang up my clothes after I wear them.

coarse (adj) - having a rough texture; unrefined manners or language
course (n) - the path something takes; a series of acts, events, or lessons
>His coarse table manners bothered his mother.
>The architect wanted a coarse finish on the walls of the building.
>The pilot plotted a course from Los Angeles to New York.
>There are six lessons in my driving course.

continual (adj) - continuing indefinitely in time
continuous (adj) - uninterrupted pattern
>The space probe sent a continual signal back to Earth.
>The car alarm let out a continuous beep until I turned it off.

could have - verb phrase showing a possibility
could of - incorrect; do not use the preposition *of* in place of the helping verb *have*
>correct - I could have seen the eclipse better with a telescope.
>incorrect - I could of seen the eclipse better with a telescope.

council (n) - a group of elected or appointed advisors
counsel (n) - advice given, especially by an expert; a lawyer
counsel (v) - to give advice
>The governor appointed a council to advise her about environmental issues.
>His counsel was reasonable; I will follow his suggestions.
>Students will have advisors to counsel them about their class schedules.

dear (adj) - cherished
deer (n) - an animal
>My grandmother's ring is very dear to me.
>Deer often cross this road in the evening.

desert (n) - a large area of dry, barren land
desert (v) - to leave a post or position of responsibility without permission
dessert (n) - a sweet course served at the end of a meal
>We will cross miles of desert on our trip from California to Texas.
>He was tried for deserting his post during the battle.
>We ordered strawberry pie for dessert.

die (n) - a six-sided cube marked with a number (1-6) on each face; plural *dice*
die (v) - to stop living; to extinguish
dye (v) - to change the color of
>In this game, we only need one die.
>We let the fire die out completely before we left the camp.
>I plan to dye this sweater black.

disinterested (adj) - not engaged; having lost interest in
uninterested (adj) - having no interest in
>After playing the game so many times, he became disinterested in it.
>When I asked her to join our club, I could tell she was uninterested.

effect - (see *affect, effect*)

emigrate - leave one's home country to live in another country
immigrate - enter a new country with the purpose of living there permanently
>In the hope of a better life, my grandfather decided to emigrate
>from his native land.
>Thousands of people immigrate to the United States each year.

envelop (v) - to wrap in a covering; to surround entirely
envelope (n) - a flat paper container
>The coastline was enveloped in fog.
>Inside the envelope was a beautiful hand-made card.

everybody - (see *anybody*)

everywhere - (see *anywhere*)

famous - renown; celebrated
infamous - having a bad or evil reputation
notorious - generally known, often for unfavorable things
>The famous rock star was greeted by an adoring crowd.
>Fast Fingers Fred, the infamous jewel thief, was last seen in Germany.
>Jesse James was a notorious criminal.

farther (adv) - at a greater distance; more remote
further (adv) - to a greater degree; extending beyond
further (v) - to advance; promote
> How much farther do we have to go?
> I will need to study the question further before I give you an answer.
> She went on to college to further her education.

fewer - refers to a number; use when items can be counted
less - refers to an amount; use when quantity can be measured
> This year's seventh grade has fewer students than last year.
> I found less information for my report than I thought I would.

formally (adv) - in a formal manner or according to customs
formerly (adv) - in past times
> The award was formally presented by the queen.
> This house was formerly a carriage house before it was remodeled.

good (adj) - fine, pleasant, favorable; use to modify a noun
well (adj) - having good health
well (adv) - in a good manner; use to modify a verb
> We saw a good documentary on television last night.
> I hope you feel well soon.
> The gymnasts performed well in the Olympics.

had of - incorrect (see *of*)

heal (v) - to cure or make well
heel (n) - the back of a foot or shoe; the ends of a loaf of bread
heel (v) - to walk behind
> The doctor said my wound should heal in a few days.
> The heel of my shoe always wears out before the rest of the shoe.
> My new puppy is learning to heel.

hear (v) - to get sound through the ear; pay attention to; try a legal case
here (adv) - in this place
> I can hear your stereo through the wall.
> The judges will hear the lawyer's argument next week.
> Please put the groceries here on the counter.

heir - a person who inherits money, property, a title, or office
air (n) - a combination of gases such as oxygen; the appearance of a quality
air (v) - to expose to air for drying or freshening
> When the will was read, I learned I was my uncle's only heir.
> The air in the room smells like the cookies you just baked.
> The violinist has an air of elegance when she plays.
> When we arrived at the cabin, we opened all the windows to air it out.

hole - a cavity, opening, or empty space
whole - the entire amount of something
> You need to dig a large hole to plant a tree this size.
> I erased my paper so much, I made a hole in it.
> We were so hungry, we ate the whole pizza.

immigrate - (see *emigrate, immigrate*)

its - belonging to it
it's - contraction for *it is*
> The mountain was so high, its peak was hidden in the clouds.
> It's time to leave for the airport.

knew (v) - past tense of *know*
new (adj) - recent occurrence, experience, or relationship; recently made or born
> I knew you would be here on time.
> We got three new students in our class today.
> I went to the hospital to see my new sister.

know (v) - to learn or understand
no (adv) - used to express a negative value or complete lack of something
> I need to know the fifty states for the test this Friday.
> Do you know how to fix the pencil sharpener?
> We had no milk in the refrigerator.

last (adj) - after all others
last (n) - the final one in a series
last (v) - to remain over a period of time
latest (adj) - the most recent
> She was the last batter in the game.
> The star pitcher said this game would be his last.
> How long did the movie last?
> This is the latest edition of the newspaper.

later (adj) - more late
later (adv) - after a set period of time
latter (adj) - the second of two groups, ideas, or things

        I was late for school, but Gina was later.
        The movie will come out later than expected.
        Of the two plans, I prefer the latter.

lay - to put down; to place an object
lay - past tense of *lie*
lie - to recline; place oneself down in a horizontal position
        Please lay your books on the desk.
        I was so tired, I lay down on the couch and fell asleep.
        As soon as I get home, I plan to lie on my bed and take a nap.

lead (v) - to guide
lead (n) - the front position; a metallic element
led (v) - past tense of *lead*

        The park ranger will lead the way.
        Our football team had the lead at half-time.
        The path led out of the park.

learn - to study or gain knowledge
teach - to instruct; to cause someone to know
        It is fun to learn a second language.
        At the driving school, the instructors teach methods of safe driving.

leave - may not be used in place of *let*
let - to allow
        Let me see your new computer.

less - (see *fewer, less*)

like - use before nouns and pronouns
as - use before phrases and clauses

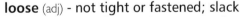

        She wanted to be a doctor like her father.
        The sky isn't as bright now as in the evening.
        We went to Hawaii this year as we had planned.

loose (adj) - not tight or fastened; slack
lose (v) - to misplace or lose possession of
loss (n) - the result of losing something
        The rope is too loose to hold the pinata in its place.
        Don't lose your tickets for the movie.
        The electrical blackout caused a loss of power for two hours.

miner (n) - a person who works in a mine to get ore
minor (adj) - of less importance or size; a musical scale
minor (n) - a person who has not reached the age of adulthood
> During the Gold Rush, his great-great-grandfather came to California to be a miner.
> Before he became a baseball star, he played in the minor leagues.
> The minor key gives this ballad a feeling of sadness.
> My plane ticket cost less because I am still a minor.

moral (adj) - ethical; relating to principles of right actions and ideas
moral (n) - the stated lesson or principle of a story
morale (n) - the level of enthusiasm or spirit of a person or group
> The practices of her company reflect her high moral standards.
> The fables of Aesop all end in a moral.
> The coach boosted the morale of his team during his half-time talk.

new - *(see knew, new)*

nowhere - (see *anywhere*)

of - do not use the preposition *of* with other prepositions such as *inside, off, outside*
> correct - inside the room
> incorrect - inside of the room
of - do not use *of* as a helping verb in place of *have*
> correct - I should have been there when you called.
> incorrect - I should of been there when you called.

or - a conjunction indicating a choice; may be used with *either*
nor - a conjunction indicating a negative choice; used with *neither*
> You can order a hot dog or a hamburger.
> We can either stay home and watch
> television or go to a movie.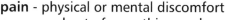
> I can neither run nor jump with this sprained ankle.

pain - physical or mental discomfort
pane - a sheet of something such as glass
> He took medicine to ease the pain of the wound.
> The broken window pane can be replaced.

passed (v) - past tense of *pass*
past (adj) - describing a time before the present
past (n) - a period of time that has already occurred
past (prep) - beyond

> We passed the freeway exit and had to go back.
> We study the history of past civilizations.
> In the past, we used to celebrate our birthdays together.
> Our house is located three blocks past the school.

peace - harmony, lack of conflict or hostility
piece - part of a whole

> The artist enjoyed the peace and quiet of the early morning.
> Who ate the last piece of pie?

plain (adj) - simple, clear, undecorated
plain (n) - a large area of flat level land
plane (n) - a flat surface; airplane

> The actress wore a plain black gown to the award ceremony.
> Pioneers built homesteads on the Great Plains.
> We took a plane to New York and then rented a car for the rest of the trip.

poor (adj) - having little worth; of inferior quality
pore (n) - a small opening in a membrane such as skin
pore (v) - to read in a concentrated manner
pour (v) - to make something flow in a stream

> This painting is a poor copy of a Van Gogh.
> Your pores allow your skin to breathe and excrete moisture.
> The professor liked to pore over ancient scrolls.
> Will you please pour me a glass of milk?

principal (adj) - most important
principal (n) - person in charge of a school; an amount of money that earns interest
principle (n) - a basic rule of law or behavior; fact of nature

> The principal cause of the noise is the construction on the street.
> Our school will have a new principal next year.
> She invested the principal from her inheritance in technology stocks.
> His refusal to lie is based on principle.
> The law of gravity is a scientific principle.

precede - to go before
proceed - to begin; to move or go forward

> Your reputation precedes you.
> After you get a receipt, proceed to the cashier to get a refund.

86

quiet (adj, n) - silent; with little sound, motion, or activity
quite - to a large extent; completely
>   We enjoy the quiet nights at our mountain cabin.
>   The quiet in the classroom was broken by the ringing of the bell.
>   After eating three courses, I felt quite full.

quotation (n) - a passage of repeated text or dialogue
quote (v) - to speak or write using text from another source
>   Please include at least one quotation from the novel in your essay.
>   My professor likes to quote Shakespeare in her lectures.

raise (v) - to lift up or heighten something
rise (n) - to move upward; to get oneself up
>   The flag monitor will raise the flag each morning.
>   I plan to raise my history grade this semester.
>   How high do you think the river will rise during the flood?
>   My grandparents rise at 7:00 every morning.

real (adj) - genuine, factual
really (adv) - truly, without question; indicates a degree of certainty
>   This doll looks like a real baby.
>   I really want to work with you on this project.

regardless (prep) - in spite of
irregardless - incorrect
>   Regardless of the weather, the game will be played on Saturday.

right (adj) - correct, proper, appropriate; the opposite of *left*
rite (n) - a traditional ceremony
write (v) - to record ideas using words or symbols
>   You found the right answer to the question.
>   We read this poem each October as part of our rite of the harvest.
>   I write in my journal every evening.

scene (n) - part of a play; a particular setting
seen (v) - past participle of *see*
>   We rehearsed the third scene in Act II.
>   The sale at the mall created a scene of confusion.
>   I have seen this movie before.

seam (n) - the place where two pieces of cloth have been sewn together
seam (v) - to sew two pieces of cloth together
seem (v) - to appear to be; to give the impression of
> The seam in the shirt goes down the side.
> Can you seam these patches together for the quilt?
> The twins seem taller than the last time I saw them.

shall (v) - may be used to indicate future tense in formal or poetic writing
> From this moment forth, no one shall be permitted to speak directly to the king.

sit - to perch on the seat
set - to place an object with purpose
> My uncle likes to sit in his chair and read.
> Please set the packages on the counter.

sight (n) - vision; something that is seen; a particular scene
sight (v) - to spot or locate, possibly through an instrument like a telescope
site (n) - a location selected for a building
cite (v) - to use a quotation as proof or a reference
> He regained his sight after the operation on his eye.
> The bird club hopes to sight a peregrine falcon.
> I will show you the site of the new library.
> Be sure to cite all your sources in the bibliography of your report.

sole (adj) - the only one
sole (n) - the bottom of a foot or shoe; a type of fish
sole (v) - to put a sole on a shoe
soul (n) - spirit

> He was the sole survivor of the crash.
> I burned the sole of my foot on the hot sand.
> I ordered filet of sole for dinner.
> He was able to sole this pair of shoes and make them look like new.
> He sang with his heart and soul.

some - an indefinite number; an unknown quantity
sum - the total of all parts; the result of adding numbers
> Some people from Chicago just moved in next door.
> I just baked cookies; would you like some?
> The sum of two and two is four.

somewhere - (see *anywhere*)

stationary (adj) - not moving; fixed
stationery (n) - paper for writing
The deer stood stationary, not wanting to draw attention to itself.
The note was written on blue stationery.

steal (v) - to take illegally; to move secretly
steel (adj, n) - metal made from iron and carbon
He was caught when he tried to steal money from the bank.
Steel beams gave the building its strength.
The jeweler's tools were made of the finest steel.

take - (see *bring, take*)

than (conj) - used to make a comparison
then (adv) - at that time; following next in order
It is hotter today than yesterday.
This sweater is larger than those.
I didn't know it then, but my sister was already home.
I melted the butter and then added it to the frosting.

that, which - *That* is correct in restrictive clauses; *which* is used in nonrestrictive
clauses. When a comma can be inserted, use *which*.
The book that was on the table is now missing.
The book, which is the best I have ever read, won the literary award.

this here, that there - the words *here* and *there* are not needed
correct - This shelf is strong enough to hold that box.
incorrect - This here shelf is strong enough to hold that there box.

their (pron) - belonging or relating to them
there (adv) - in that place
there (pron) - used to introduce a sentence
they're - contraction for *they are*
Every year our neighbors take their vacation in June.
We catch the bus on the corner over there.
There were no incorrect answers on your homework.
They're going to meet us at the restaurant.

theirs (pron) - belonging to others
there's - contraction for *there is*

The books on the table are theirs.
There's only one right way to solve this problem.

threw (v) - past tense of *throw*

through (prep) - indicates movement from one point to another; in at one point and out at another point

        The quarterback threw a twenty-yard pass.

        We drove through the tunnel under the bay.

to (prep) - toward a person, place or thing

too (adv) - also, very

two - the number that is one more than one

        The principal gave the award to our class.

        May I come too?

        We don't want to swim because it is too cold.

        The two skaters raced for a mile.

vain (adj) - without success; extreme pride in oneself

vane (n) - a metal device used to show the direction of the wind

vein (n) - a blood vessel; a narrow strip of metal in rock

        We tried in vain to call you on your cell phone.

        The judges of the beauty contest felt she was too vain.

        The farmer installed a weather vane on top of his barn.

        I can see the vein in your arm.

        The vein of copper in the mine was worth millions.

wait (v) - to remain in place until something happens

weight (n) - a measure of mass; what something weighs

        My dog likes to wait for me at the bus stop.

        The nurse checked my weight before I saw the doctor.

ware (n) - manufactured item or product

wear (v) - to put on clothing; to erode or lessen the strength of something

where (adv, conj) - in or at what place

        The artists brought their wares to the street market.

        We wear our school uniforms Monday through Thursday.

        I wear out my erasers faster than my pencils.

        Where are the letters you want me to mail?

        This is the place where we first met.

way (n) - the direction or route of travel; the procedure for doing something

weigh (v) - to measure how heavy something is

        We walk to school this way every day.

        He knows the best way to build a tree house.

        The doctor's nurse wants to weigh me on each visit.

weather (n) - a description of what happens in the atmosphere, e.g. wind, rain, snow
whether (conj) - used to indicate alternative choice; often used with *or*
          I like to check the weather in a city before I travel there.
          He wasn't sure whether to go or not.

which (pron) - interrogative or relative pronoun indicating what one or ones
          (*Which* is used in nonrestrictive clauses that are set off by commas. In
          restrictive clauses, use the word *that*.)
witch (n) - a woman with magical power; sorceress
          Which shirt do you think I should wear?
          The tools, which are the only ones I used, are in the closet.
          The witch in the fairy tale put a spell on the prince.

who - subject form of the interrogative or relative pronoun indicating which person
whom - object form of *who*; used as the object of a verb or preposition
          Who will make the sandwiches for lunch?
          I met the man who will coach our soccer team.
          We didn't know whom to ask about the assignment.
          To whom did you address the letter?

who's - contraction for *who is*
whose (pron) - refers to a noun that has possession
          I wonder who's going to carry the luggage to the car.
          Whose backpack was left in the hallway?
          I will call the person whose ticket won the raffle.

will (n) - determination; a legal statement assigning property after one's death
will (v) - to intend: used generally to indicate future tense
          He has the will to succeed.
          We will meet you after dinner.

wood (n) - material in tree trunks and branches; lumber made from trees; a grove of
          trees
would (v) - to show intent or a wish; often used as a helping verb in a verb phrase
would of - incorrect; (see *of*)
          How much wood do we need to build the fence?
          I like Robert Frost's poem about walking through the wood.
          Where would you like to have dinner?

your (pron) - belonging to you
you're - contraction for *you are*
          I bought your birthday present at the mall.
          You're the new class president!

Index

Common Core State Standards Alignment

Grade Level	Common Core State Standards
Grade 5 ELA-Literacy	W.5.4 Produce clear and coherent writing in which the development and organization are appropriate to task, purpose, and audience. (Grade-specific expectations for writing types are defined in standards 1–3 above.)
	W.5.5 With guidance and support from peers and adults, develop and strengthen writing as needed by planning, revising, editing, rewriting, or trying a new approach. (Editing for conventions should demonstrate command of Language standards 1-3 up to and including grade 5 here.)
Grade 6 ELA-Literacy	W.6.4 Produce clear and coherent writing in which the development, organization, and style are appropriate to task, purpose, and audience. (Grade-specific expectations for writing types are defined in standards 1–3 above.)
	W.6.5 With some guidance and support from peers and adults, develop and strengthen writing as needed by planning, revising, editing, rewriting, or trying a new approach. (Editing for conventions should demonstrate command of Language standards 1–3 up to and including grade 6 here.)
Grade 7 ELA-Literacy	W.7.4 Produce clear and coherent writing in which the development, organization, and style are appropriate to task, purpose, and audience. (Grade-specific expectations for writing types are defined in standards 1–3 above.)
	W.7.5 With some guidance and support from peers and adults, develop and strengthen writing as needed by planning, revising, editing, rewriting, or trying a new approach, focusing on how well purpose and audience have been addressed. (Editing for conventions should demonstrate command of Language standards 1–3 up to and including grade 7 here.)
Grade 8 ELA-Literacy	W.8.4 Produce clear and coherent writing in which the development, organization, and style are appropriate to task, purpose, and audience. (Grade-specific expectations for writing types are defined in standards 1–3 above.)
	W.8.5 With some guidance and support from peers and adults, develop and strengthen writing as needed by planning, revising, editing, rewriting, or trying a new approach, focusing on how well purpose and audience have been addressed. (Editing for conventions should demonstrate command of Language standards 1–3 up to and including grade 8 here.)
Grade 9-10 ELA-Literacy	W.9-10.4 Produce clear and coherent writing in which the development, organization, and style are appropriate to task, purpose, and audience. (Grade-specific expectations for writing types are defined in standards 1–3 above.)
	W.9-10.5 Develop and strengthen writing as needed by planning, revising, editing, rewriting, or trying a new approach, focusing on addressing what is most significant for a specific purpose and audience. (Editing for conventions should demonstrate command of Language standards 1–3 up to and including grades 9–10 here.)
Grade 11-12 ELA-Literacy	W.11-12.4 Produce clear and coherent writing in which the development, organization, and style are appropriate to task, purpose, and audience. (Grade-specific expectations for writing types are defined in standards 1–3 above.)
	W.11-12.5 Develop and strengthen writing as needed by planning, revising, editing, rewriting, or trying a new approach, focusing on addressing what is most significant for a specific purpose and audience. (Editing for conventions should demonstrate command of Language standards 1–3 up to and including grades 11–12 here.).

Printed in the United States
by Baker & Taylor Publisher Services